A Little Book with Big Promises

By: Suzanne Pereira

ISBN-13: 9798739208040

Dedication

For God: Who holds and unfolds all and
for the loved ones He has blessed me with.

Table of Contents

Table of Content (continued)

Table of Contents (continued)

Foreword

What a joy it is to be writing to you! I hope that the big messages in this little book bring you some insight or reassurance of how much you are loved. The entries hold their own unique and powerful lessons. So, feel free to start at the very beginning, halfway through or to open up the pages at random to read. I have no doubt that the messages intended for you to receive will reach you. I almost hesitate to say that this book has been a collaboration between me and God, but I would be dishonest not to admit that truth. I could never write with the boldness found in some of these entries on my own. If we choose, we all can collaborate with God every day. Within the pages of this book, every thought has been accompanied by prayer. Every message blessed with pure intentions. I hope once you read some entries you will feel that truth.

The reflections I share are from my personnel experiences. I have discovered so many blessings in walking in relationship with God, that one day I just started to write them down and have never stopped. My prayer is that some of what I share will awaken promises within you that may have gotten buried and forgotten. I hope you are willing to open yourself up to a Great Remembering. A Remembering that we are a part of a great love, a great purpose, a Great God. Even if you were never told of God before you will recognize His love as you accept it and reconnect to this greater good that has been following you all your life. It will feel familiar as it has always been yours, since the beginning. As you read, I hope you feel the excitement which I felt writing every word! Thank you for your courage, openness and companionship as we read together.

The Journey in Journaling

I have always felt comfortable putting pen to paper. Truth be told, I prefer pencil to paper. Writing with pencil gives the writer a sense of carving and etching each abstract thought and potentially fleeting feeling down on to the page. If I had it my way, books would be written by the author's handwriting and sold that way. So much of the art of writing gets lost in the typewritten manuscript. Just think about how exciting it is to receive handwritten letters in the mail or greeting cards with well-wishes written inside ever so lovingly. Every twist and turn characterizes the content of the writing, truly connecting the writer to the reader. The best we can do in this modern age is to select the most appropriate font and hope the sincerity of our message is conveyed.

The process of writing itself is truly very liberating. I often kept a journal in my younger years. I remember not knowing what I wanted to write only to later discover having page after page of thoughts written down. If you have never kept a journal, you may consider beginning one. Don't feel committed to recording an entry every day or even every week. Just know that the space is there, somewhere in the house, to turn to in order to vent, release or to offer thanksgiving and praise.

Journals don't have to record deep and tawdry secrets. Nor should they contain grocery list or, worse yet, “to do” lists. Rather journals should contain random entries, stories, memories and feelings, revelations and affirmations. The words at times may be hardly legible. You see sometimes it matters very little if the words you write will ever be read again, it is simply that they have been written. Your wishes, prayers, hurts and dreams have found a place outside of yourself. They have been shared and materialized in a safe and loving manner.

At first you may feel much like I did; that you have nothing to say. Begin then by writing just that, “I feel like I have nothing to say…”. Inevitably words will follow, then sentences, paragraphs until eloquent soliloquies result. Don't concern yourself with grammar, punctuation or spelling. Those are limitations the world has placed on speech. Often the emotions of the heart are too wild for structure. Just let it all out. Let the spirit move you to feel, thank and articulate. For most of us it has been far too long. Why let negative emotions fester to a point where illness and disease erode us? Let those toxic emotions out through written expression. You will discover that they will disappear, leaving you liberated. You may feel tired at times so stop often. Don't worry your words will still be there when you choose to return to them. The beauty of writing is that you can never be silenced.

Soon your entries will become more positive, insightful and even joyful. For you will be as well. You will be healing. The anger, hostility, stress and tension of the past will become a memory and it will have been replaced by clarity, forgiveness and hope. Challenges and trying times will return but now you are well armed with the perfect weapon - your writing. It shall diffuse the rising anxiety. It will decrease the fear and eliminate the loneliness. You will find solace in the pages as you write. Words will be your companion, your validation and more.

During this process you may wonder to whom it is that you write. To different people on different occasions, I suppose the answer will be. You will write to your true self, to your younger self, older self, to those living and to those pasted on as well. You will write to the angels and to God Himself. The recipient of these letters may be different but the wrier always the same. The many facets of who you are and of what you are capable of being will be revealed. At times the poet will emerge sprouting rhythmic couplets and sonnets. The musician in you will compose lyrics to beautiful songs. The clown or comic will have humorous anecdotes to deliver and the philosopher questions to ask an attempt to answer. Always it will be you, wise and wonderful you.

So take time to nourish your soul. Let the tears flow as you write as well as the laughter, sighs and dreams. Always write at your own pace and in your own words. Enjoy. Don't fear judgment or criticism as you write. God has already read your story. Nothing shocks Him. Remember He has read your heart and considers it a best-seller!

Music therapy

It is amazing how music could change the atmosphere in a room and attitude in the heart. There have been times when I came home from work tired and literally falling off my feet but decided to turn on the radio. I couldn't believe how the music soothed me. To my surprise the lyrics of most of the songs automatically came to mind and escaped my lips. I was delighted by this remembering. My breathing became relaxed and fluid while my whole body slowly began to unwind. Once achy and clenched, my muscles stretched out now long and strong. My mind cleared and I became fresh again.

Slower songs rocked me in my seat while faster once had my toes and fingers tapping. I often try this technique whenever I feel exhausted or pushed to fatigue. It is more fruitful than binge watching television or other mindless distractions. I remember times when I sat for hours watching nothing of significance on my computer screen or telephone and eating whatever I had at hand. Not remembering episodes or what I had tasted. However, the times when I chose to let music fill my house everything changed. Sad songs released the tears I didn't even know I needed to cry. The faster melodies brought out moves I never knew I had! My heart beat to the rhythm and I let my body follow. It didn't matter if I looked good. I felt good. I felt light and little and free. Just by turning on the music, I was able to access magic, a sweet healing magic. I hope the next time you feel at the end of your rope you turn on some tunes and tango ‘till you are transformed!

Sweet sleep

Sleep, what a wonderful gift. Have you ever really thought about it? What a retreat from the movement of the world and the constant noise in our minds. I am forever a fan of sleep. My mother often had bouts of insomnia when I was growing up and I remember how grateful she was when rare nights of sleep graced her pillow. She taught me to appreciate the sanctity of sleep and the need and necessity of slumber.

Have you ever wondered why we were created for this need to sleep? I mean despite the obvious physiological reasons, why were we not created to stay awake 24/7 and just keep going and going? My guess is that God needed a guaranteed time when He could have us all to Himself. A time when we are at peace with our emotions. When we are free from wondering what move to make next, how to interpret this or how to analyze that. Sleep is a time when our bodies are at rest; are limbs still, our hearts and our breathing smooth.

I sometimes imagine sleeping like I did as a child in my crib or in my parents loving arms. Lying flat on my stomach with my cheek smooshed up against the mattress, really connects me to that safe feeling and warm comfort of my younger years. I imagine I am in the embrace of a loved one once again, who holds me as I sleep. How warm, little and cared for I feel. Whenever I watch a baby sleep, I envy their surrender. I could watch them for hours and long to escape as they do.

I am convinced that we do not age as we sleep, although I have no scientific proof of that. Instead, we rejuvenate our organs as well as our spirit. Perhaps our bodies go into a kind of rebalancing and adjustment. If left to wake up naturally without the aid of an alarm, how do we know when to wake up? Whose hand gently stirs us awake? The same mystery applies to when we fall asleep. How is it that we do not remember drifting into sleep? Does a switch go off, do our batteries expire or does a gentle whisper call our name to rest?

Let's learn to truly savor this sanctuary. Make a ritual out of sleep time. Prepare by dimming the lights of the house and slipping into a favourite pair of pyjamas. Lift the covers of your bed to reveal fresh clean linens and soft bouncy pillows. Then lift the shades and open the curtains to your bedroom window. Don't worry it's dark now, let the wish filled stars in the heavens watch over you. Lie still, then stretch out until you find your sweet spot on the mattress. You'll be smiling by now and often that is prayer enough. Let your heart speak whatever you have left to say for the day. Then let the Lord wrap His arms around you cradling you, back and forth. Can you feel His breath and hear His heart beating? Now you only have to close your eyes to see His face.

The Rich Stillness

It is one of those beautiful winter nights tonight. The evening sky is clearing to reveal crisp stars. I have come to accept the cold wind chill my native Canada throws at us. The house is quiet as I write except for the ticking of the clock and the hum of the furnace. It is so important to value these times when all is well with family and friends. When our bodies are free of severe pain and our minds are clear. How easily lost this blessed moment could become with the buzz of the phone or the ring of the doorbell. Maybe even we ourselves choose to break the magic. In confusing such restful times with loneliness, laziness or boredom we can be convinced to turn on the television or shuffle with some menial task or chore. We have to learn to be still and capture these precious rich moments that grace us. Busier lives do not equate to fuller lives.

We are warm enough, fed enough, safe enough and loved enough. Counting blessings only at Christmas time and Thanksgiving is really just sad. If we learn to capture these surprise moments of peace and stillness, we are truly appreciative of our Creator. Living with this awareness will bring a joy of its own. We become open to reflection and an awareness will follow. We can be still enough to have our blessings settle upon us. We can validate the miracles of every breath, heartbeat, moment and memory. Miracles can otherwise go unnoticed without these reflective times. Too often in our society of “surround sounds” and big screens, we can get caught up in the unnecessary fireworks of things. Why live louder when we know that the sweetest words are often spoken in a whisper.

Walking Within

" The other day while going for a walk ... ". How many times have you spoken these words or have heard someone else speak these words? They can sometimes be followed by a funny anecdote, some revelation or observation. It would appear as if the mere act of going for a stroll can elicit a memory, inspiration and even alter a mood. I have been trying to go for a walk regardless of the season for at least 30 to 45 minutes a day. Sometimes I plug into a podcast and other times I may be connecting with a friend over the phone. However, it is during the times when I simply just walk that have been most blessed.

It is during these “wide-open” walks where I have nothing distracting me that I have been able to really invite God along. He is everywhere. He is in the blending of the branches of the trees that tower before me as the wind blows. He is in the darting birds that thread their way in between houses, wires and tree limbs. He is in the cracks in the pavement telling stories of weathering, erosion and survival. God is in this perfect Stillness.

Suddenly I am aware of a special type of quiet. The type of quiet that is absent of voices, internal and external ones. It is during these moments that I could truly pay reverence to our Creator. I can hold out my hand so He could hold it while we walk. I could open up my heart and my lungs so I could breathe in the Spirit and have it circulated throughout all of me. I begin to walk as if I am walking not towards something nor away from something but just within something. Within a great love and a great understanding that I was created for such a time as this. That despite any worldly obligations I first have an obligation to recognize that this space and time will never come back again. It is sacred. The tilt of the sun in the sky, the temperature, the balance of nutrients in the air and in the soil. The earth’s position within our solar system is just perfectly aligned as it should be. The stars may not be out if I walk during the day, but I still know that they're there and the vast heavens above me suddenly become a protective umbrella. I discover resources that are around me and at the same time within me.

When I hit this sweet spot when I know I have chosen wisely and have been blessed with peace of mind and joy of heart, I am humbled to tears. I am excited to discover how long this energy will last and I do my best to praise, to honour and to appreciate the gift. I know soon, with the demands of the world, as well as my call to serve, that this special blessed walk with God will have to end. But I don't begin to get disheartened. I actually feel its invigoration and trust that these moments will come again. The tears released have created space for clarity. The deep breaths have aired out the staleness of stress. These moments have nourished me and provided me with what I need during my upcoming times of serving.

My wish for you is that you can be still enough to walk this way. I pray that you are open enough to close off everything that doesn't matter. I'm excited as I complete this message because I know for some of you, you will drop this book immediately and go out searching for what I have described. How happy I am that you will find it.

Believe you can fly

Slums, we all get them. You know those dark and dreary moments when things just seem to be, well, wrong. We get hit hard it seems, by gloom and we sink quickly into its trap. Our attentions turn to quick fixes like; fast-food, binge episode watching or online shopping. We neglect those we love, and we don't do our exercises. Our expressions changed as well, we frown and even the tone of our voice drops. Our eyes and shoulders droop and legs tremble. Physically we betray our bodies, but this betrayal begins mentally. If we are not careful, we continue to spiral downwards into a land of lost and lonely thoughts.

Think back upon the last time you ever felt as down as I just described. Next, think about how it passed. Did a knight on a white horse ride up and slay all your dragons? Did you win the lottery and buy your problems off? Did you cope wisely, or did you wallow in your misery feeling sorry for yourself? How did that work for you? Not very well I bet. I know because I've been there. I have also been the hostess of one too many pity parties. But we're better than that! Ultimately, we lived through it and it passed! It takes a little faith and a whole lot of spirit, but it can be done.

Actually, it must be done and done quickly. The key is in the quickness. As soon as we get a whiff of the dread begin to want to creep in, we declare it is not for us, not today, not any day. "Today is the day the Lord has made, and we will rejoice and be glad in it". (Psalm 118:24). You see God did not leave us alone or unarmed for challenges such as these. He has left us His powerful Words. We have reminders, proclamations, reassurances throughout the Bible of our victory in Christ. Take courage in the words of Psalm 37, verse 23-24 for example:

"The Lord guides the man in the way he should go
And protects those who please him.
If they fall, they will not stay down,
Because the Lord will help them up." (Psalm 37: 23-24).

The next time negative feelings or words begin to fester take a timeout. Stop before this funk penetrates your whole perception. Stop before it penetrates outwardly on to your family and friends. You see we are that powerful. We are that necessary in life. By stopping, you alter yourself. Speak powerful words of God over your life. If you've ever had to train a dog and get him or her back on track, you will remember that you speak a command followed by a little nudge of redirection. This helps the dog refocus and collect itself, switch gears, change channels and take initiative. These same principles can apply to us as well. Speak a command over our lives and redirect ourselves.

Switching our focus to our basic needs may help. Eat well. Avoid harmful misleading energy “fixes”. Instead nourish your body with fresh and whole foods that smell and taste healing. A healthcare professional will best be able to help you here should there be some sort of vitamin deficiency or other area of concern that might need to be addressed. Exercise if given the ok to do so. Walking or a few stretches with deep cleansing breaths can get you motivated. This will get the ball rolling in the right direction - up words! Once again consult your doctor before changing or entering into any kind of exercise program for best results.

Find your release. If you need to write out your junk, write until the trash translates to poetry. If you need to paint, splash around the canvas until your strokes create a masterpiece. If you need to sing, squeal until the voices of angels accompany you. If you need to run, run away until you run towards. If you need to connect, give until you receive.

The point in all of this is to refuse to surrender. Be victorious! Let the threat against your good call up greatness within you. Believe that the mountains themselves could be moved and blown away. You will sleep well after such hard work, but it will be a tranquil rest. Those who love you will have been spared the pain of possible hostility that could have otherwise resulted. The world was saved from any added toxicity. Instead, you have yet another example of the resilience that is part of your testimony. You will have experienced the miracle of the grace that is God’s gift to us and the love that overturns all evil and transforms it for our good.

Thank you for Healing Me

When was the last time you celebrated your house, the headache that went away, the cramps or pain that dissipated? How about rejoicing over a scab that clotted and protected? Once we begin to feel better after being ill, we so often say, "Oh I feel so much better, the antibiotics/medicine must be working." That is only part of the story. God has been working. That is the truth after all, really. The truth is that God does the healing. He is ever caring and attentive. I am not saying to stop taking your vitamins or medicine. I am saying it is important to acknowledge the truth of God's healing hand in all of our affliction.

There is a medical clinic close to where I live. Sometimes when I drive by late at night, I could see people in the waiting room through the windows. I say a prayer for those inside, for not long ago I too sat waiting, scared, sick and wondering. Then I say a prayer of gratitude for God having healed me and for His continual source of light to heal.

There are times after a doctor's visit that we whine about their advice to us. We complain about doctor's orders to stop smoking, eat healthier and to exercise more. In our ungratefulness we forget others who would gladly trade our diagnosis for theirs. We gripe and complain about these recommendations or restrictions but how many other people have been told there is little that can be done to improve their health? They would gladly trade places with us. During trials when you may be tempted to become discouraged or anxious remember the legacy left for us. The legacy of men walking on water, of lepers healed, of blind people regaining their sight, of thousands being fed with a few loaves of bread and fish, of mistakes forgiving and of death denied.

Let us honour these past miracles and welcome the new ones. Imagine doing this wonderful thing for someone and they just thinking it was a coincidence or luck. God works countless miracles of protection and healing every day, privately. Let's learn to give credit to Him. I have a scar on my hand from a bicycle accident I had a couple of years ago and when I gather my hands to pray, I sometimes notice it. It serves as a reminder. It recalls the trouble but more importantly, it recalls the rescue, the healing. It is no coincidence that mark landed on my hand. It continues to serve me best there. We have been spared countless disasters most of which we may never know about. Let our scars and the scars of the cross remind us of our deliverance and our blessings. Celebrate every movement we can make, every sight we can see, every thought we retain and every night of peaceful sleep. Let us say, “Thank you, God, I remember what You've done and rejoice in the wonders yet to come from your healing and loving hands”.

Discernment

One of my biggest struggles has been to know when to be still and when to act. Decisions can be the hardest thing we have to make. When I was a child's I thought making pancakes must be hard, now that I am older I long for those days when my goal was to master simple tasks and new skills. Discernment? Now there's the real rocket science.

We wonder about so many choices we are faced with daily. Do I give this person another chance? Do I make this career change? Should I reach out or do I give them space? Some decisions can be approached in a very pragmatic and linear manner. Pros and cons list often help us come to the most practical conclusion. We can weigh the odds, calculate percentages and consult professionals and advisors. But it is the most personal and sensitive decisions that require a much higher referral. For discernment, we want to make sure we are being led by the Spirit and nothing else.

God alone can council best in matters of the heart. He is always available, easily accessible and ever-loving. In fact, He already knows what it is that is troubling us. He knows our torment, our indecisiveness and our insecurities. He understands our torn hearts and tired minds. Before anything God offers His Unconditional Love. Just what we need when we feel panic and uncertainty creeping in on us. He knows our intentions, our hopes and feels for our predicament.

At times when I am most confused as to what position to take or road to follow, I come, as a child, running into God's loving embrace. He knows my sorrow. He knows my guilt for troubling Him when others have far heavier burdens. He is honoured that it is Him I choose to turn to. I get quiet and still. Immediately I feel His presence. He is there right by my side, listening, waiting and soothing. I ask all the questions I want. Still, He remains. I cry, I shout, I sing, I am silent and all along He is my peace.

I turn my focus to Him and find Him in everything. I recognized Him in the night sky or the sun's rays through my window. I hear His song in my prayers or as I read scripture. I feel His love in the warmth that envelops my heart and squeezes the tears from my eyes. Then, when I am ready to receive His guidance, I listen. The answers begin to come through inspiration, ideas, in remembering, or in a message whispered to my heart. The answers are always accompanied by a feeling of peace. A constant message of peace, to trust in Him and to remember who I am in Him. It is with the same final plea that I always end my meditation during these once restless episodes. I pray that I will never be misled again by myself or circumstances. I accept that I am exactly where He needs me to be, that I am loved and that everything will be alright.

Always, Always Remember Who You Are

Intimidation. What an ugly tactic in a coward's game. Have you ever felt intimidated? I pray that you never feel that way again. Who was it that intimidated you? A bully, a boss, a stranger, a “friend”? Who are they to intimidate you? I don't blame them really; they don't know who you are. But you do. You know that you are a child of the Almighty God.

You are His handiwork. You are filled with His love and goodness. Now how could you ever feel intimidated again?

Do you accept this description of yourself? If not, it doesn't make it any less true. You are that important you know. You are that loved and cherished. You are that beautiful and holy. Others who use silly tactics or cruel words don't know any better. But you do. They may be lost, but you remain certain. They may be disillusioned but you remain clear. They may not have things figured out yet, but you have been told the good news and believe. Recognize their limitations are not your own. With God all things are possible. God sees with the heart what other see with the limited vision out of their eyes.

Why shrivel up when you were created to bloom? Why hide when you were created to shine? Do you avoid greatness so others around you will not feel threatened or insecure? Let them feel whatever God needs them to feel. Let Him tug at their hearts through their envy of you. Let them be forced to examine themselves when their attempt to knock you down fails. Reflect the pain back to where it could do good, its original source. Let their sour words and angry emotions boomerang back to their hardened hearts and begin to cause a crack.

Keep in mind God's words from the beautiful Sermon on the Mount:

“Happy are you when people insult you and persecute you and tell all kinds of evil eyes against you because you are my followers. Be happy and glad, for a great reward is kept for you in heaven.” (Matthew 511 - 12).

Now doesn't that help. Read it again, read it often. Carry it with you and your heart and have it become your encouragement through difficult interactions. I pray that it will be the secret you possess that brings a confident smile to your face when it's hard to do so. Ultimately, it is love that prevails. God is proud of you. Never believe otherwise and never settle for believing any less.

Why do bullies bully? Because you have something they want. They see peace and want a part; they see joy and long for that freedom. They see love and feel lonely in the shadows. You will teach them it is possible. You will prove it can be real. They will want to be more like you, unshaken and faithful. They will see in you an alternative to the life they have dragged along year after year beat up, tired and desolate. They will see it in your resilience and confidence. Remaining still when the storm arises will amaze even the harshest critics. The good that lives inside them will begin to find a foothold. It will keep them up at night. It will cause them to hunger for the only thing that truly satisfies-God. You may be a part of their journey and they may be a test on yours. Make sure you serve them well while you pass the test.

Good for the soul

One day not too long ago I was so angry at someone. They were determined to hurt me for whatever reason; they're garbage, not mine. I remember, well I guess I don't remember the anger I felt. Isn't that funny? I know I felt angry because I remember praying to God to take the anger away but reflecting back on the situation now, I can't even feel a drop of that pain. How completely God healed me. How completely He always heals.

I remember driving when I had asked him to take my anger away praying," Lord I feel so angry. Please, I know I can do nothing good with this. Take it away." Just then, right in my car, the thought entered my mind to occupy my day with as many good deeds as I could. I literally and figuratively turned off the road I was on and headed towards my grandmother's nursing home to pay her a visit. Once there I marvelled at her energy and spirit as I sat across from this 95-year-old woman; a mother of 10, grandmother of 23 and great-grandmother of 21! (Now that sentence deserves an exclamation mark if ever a sentence deserved one.) She didn't stop talking as she prepared herself for dinner, slipping on her good shoes to enter the dining room with what resembled graceful yoga moves. I marvelled at her as I watched and listened in respect. We giggled and reconnected. She thanked me for coming and told me she enjoyed the visit but I am sure I gained more from our time together than she did.

My next stop brought me to the nearby bookstore. I perused the aisles until I came to the gift card section. There I found a sweet card that reminded me of a co-worker who was going through a hard time of her own lately. I purchase a little angel pin to include inside the envelope. She later caught me attempting to hide the present by her car in the parking lot at work. We laughed when she nearly gave me a heart attack when she unlocked her doors from a distance causing the car's lights to blink horn to "bleep, bleep". Since I was busted, I confess my plan to drop off her little gift undetected. We shared a chuckle over my mischievousness and still recall that encounter ever once and a while.

Later that same day, driving home from work, for whatever reason I found myself taking a longer route home. Well to my surprise I noticed a sign out on the front lawn of a church advertising a rummage sale. This was a bonus indeed! The sale was due to start in 30 minutes. Immediately a friend of mine who is a fellow garage sale enthusiast popped into my mind. I called her up and offered to drive her to the sale admitting that it was very last minute. She jumped at the offer and we later laughed at our excitement over the worn-out curtains and rusty old TV trays that we had purchased and how they brought us so much joy!

What I didn't know was that she had been having some stressful family issues of her own to deal with on that day and was able to forget them for a while. My phone call was a much-needed escape which led to indulging in some treasure hunting retail therapy.

It had become clear to me as the day progressed that the earlier anger I had felt had disappeared and my mood was light and sunny again. My joy was back! The three ladies I connected with that the day had been a part of my healing and restoration. I hope somehow, I was a similar blessing to them. It appears that once I decided to let the anger out there remained a whole lot more room for God. What one person had initially intended for bad I beautified into good – a true goodness. With God's help the anger was gone and victory was mine again.

Honour Your Covenant

A friend of mine once came to me so frustrated by the corruption and dishonesty of others around her that she contemplated quitting her job and starting over. After I let her finish her rant, I simply asked her, "And so, would you trade your life for theirs?" She quietly answered, “No”. The stress and heaviness once on her face was soon replaced with clarity and calm. She sighed as her peace returned and she was back on track once again. I think I was able to help her because I also remember moments of frustration when I witnessed things like; the unjust treatment of others, never-ending lies, phoniness and deceit. But one Sunday, heavy with these emotions I heard a story that changed everything.

I recall going to church with some of the residue of a negative work environment still stuck to me. Thankfully I remained present enough during worship to realize the Bible story being reviewed that day was extremely pertinent to what I was currently living. The story describes a hard worker who was upset by the laziness of a fellow co-worker. Much like myself and my dear friend, this frustrated worker was angered to find that at the end of the workday both he and the slacking employee were paid the exact same wage. When the annoyed employee approached his employer about this grievance, the employer shocked him with his response. The wise boss confirmed with his loyal employee that the work agreement they shared had not been violated. The two had agreed to an adequate amount of pay for hours worked and duties performed. What the lazy co-worker was paid or not paid did not take away from the initial contract the employer had made with the good worker. (This is the paraphrasing of the parable entitled, The Workers in the Vineyard, in Matthew 20: 1-16).

Sitting in the pew hearing this account made my jaw drop. I was immediately humbled by the parable and amazed at how a passage written thousands of years ago still held such significance today. The truth in that tale resonated with me and peace quickly replace the disdain and resentment that had troubled me earlier. I reflected on my "agreement" with my employer. I was paid for a certain number of hours worked and duties performed. No more, no less. I had honoured that commitment. Furthermore, I was fortunate in my employment and enjoyed my work.

I then reminded myself of my "agreement" with God. I was to keep my own moral compass properly tuned. I was to run my own race. I was not to steal nor stress over money. I am to keep my eyes on more precious gifts, enjoy beauty that was placed before me, and appreciate the health of my body and the ones I love. With God's help I am to serve with joy at all times. I am to give thanks for my blessings and trust that I will be continually given what I need to be a blessing to others. This was my covenant with God.

Once I remembered what my covenant was, I was able to reassess the important areas of my life that required my energies. I was determined to hold my end of the bargain and was only pleased to do so. Frustration and offense can only distract us from our goals. It is a clever tool used to keep us off track. Don't let this waste of precious power be how you address injustices, corruption, greed or hate. Nourish your covenant. Stand strong in your beliefs. Know the ultimate truth that God is just and ever watching. Nurture the preciousness of your duties. Keep yourself strong, focussed and ready to receive the blessings that your covenant promises. Your attitude should be one of incorruptibility, regardless of your circumstances and environment.

God understands it isn't always easy but with every decision not to get involved in drama, gossip, conflict and wrongdoing it does become easier. I'm excited to think of how your life will change with these words of advice. I am happy in the belief that you will not be distracted so easily from the good works God has planned for you to perform. Nor will you be as tempted to abandon your life of clean living. Your health will improve. Your attitude will lighten. Your mind will clear up and strengthen. And your covenant will be renewed and its commitment blessed.

"Be still, and know that I am God" (Psalms 46:10)

Sometimes there are days when nothing seems to be going right. It feels like there is a pressure that seems to be closing in. The news reports about wars, climate change, crime and other dangers. Neighbours and co-workers inform you of the latest story of doom and gloom. You yourself begin to feel heavy-hearted and pessimistic. It's times like these that we need to stop the voices. Turn off the television, turn down the radio, fast from social media, excuse yourself from the bubbles of drama and just as important; silence the negative self-talk within your mind. Times like these calls for an immediate return to God. Draw close to Him so that His Voice be the only voice to come through.

I am reminded one of these times of struggle and the deliverance that came through in a special way. My heart hurt and my dreams were being tested. I had been pushing and pulling, kicking and screaming to get my life right and just needed a win. Frustration exhausted me. I couldn't even find the words to pray. I collapse down under my bedroom window and remember saying, “If only I knew you loved me.” Just then a quiet surrounded me. My limbs were still and my breathing slow. The calm made it feel like I was about to drift off into sleep when I heard the voice of a man say, "Remember, I love you.” I know! Wow! That's what I thought too what was happening. Call the Vatican! Could this be real? Did I really hear that? Seconds later, I heard a car door close and a car drive away. When I looked outside my window, my neighbour was standing outside his house waving goodbye to his grandson as his family drove off. The words I had heard must have been his affectionate goodbye to his grandchild. But I know they were also much more. God had used that declaration as a message for me, I have no doubt.

That moment was such a powerful affirmation of God’s love for me. Imagine hearing just what you need to hear when you needed to hear it. I can't even tell you how I felt; humbled, loved, understood and cared for. Of course, we can’t treat our faith like magic, expecting answers to arrive with the wave of a wand or the snap of a finger. Faith is more precious than that. It requires stillness, vulnerability, gratitude and belief. The hardest of these for me has always been the stillness part. Patience does not come naturally to me but I'm learning. I'm stubborn as well and that probably doesn't help matters. But excuses aside, I have now learned that I am most tempted to rush, run and produce when the very thing I'm being called to do is to wait, stop and be still. Had I not pressed pause on that day I would have missed God's message of love to me through my neighbor's love for his grandson.

The times in our lives when we hit the wall with no more tears to cry, God waits for the stillness. He waits to speak. His voice is not rushed or loud. His tone never anxious, authoritative or fearful. It is calm, loving and true. It can be felt in the spirit and heard in the heart. I hope everyone stops and chooses to return to that quiet place where peace lives. Where fear and panic dissipate. Where all is familiar and safe. Where God waits for us to come and visit.

It's Okay They'll Still Love You

Have you known that horrible feeling when you put your foot in your mouth or have been just a little too short with someone you love? We've all done it, I'm sure. It's just an awful feeling, isn't it? You feel like the biggest idiot. You tell yourself, “If only I had more patience, just held my tongue or been a little more compassionate." But you weren't, for whatever reason you crossed the line and hurt someone dear to you unintentionally. The good news is it is not too late to be all those things you should have been.

Having said this, before reaching out to the one you have offended and asking for their forgiveness; take a quick inventory of how *you* are feeling. Maybe you had a bad day or maybe you're carrying a little baggage or hostility that you need to get rid of before making your next move. Heal yourself before attempting to heal another. There was a reason why you lost your peace so honour yourself enough to address it. Remember your heart. Remember you are kind and good. A close friend told me once if you stay in regret, you are admitting you do not like who you are. Yes, there may be behaviours or actions you are not proud of but remember that you are a good person in order to move on. You genuinely care about others otherwise you wouldn't feel so bad about letting them down. You reacted in a moment of weakness, now is the time to get strong again so you could be true to yourself and there for another.

Have something good to eat, soak in the tub or go for a walk to clear your head and your whole body. Exhale and forgive yourself, then and only then, come back to your sister, mother, friend, husband, wife, child, whomever and let them know you wished you could have been more help earlier. They love you. They'll forgive you and understand. If they need some time and space, respect that. Do not be tempted to see it as a form of punishment towards you but as a form of healing for themselves.

Sometimes a short note or greeting card may be appropriate. It may help to extend the olive branch and reopen the lines of communication. Whichever approach you choose, lead with your heart. The pain you feel for making a mistake should never extend into condemnation. We know enough not to judge others and yet we often forget to show ourselves the same courtesy. What happened could very well be growing pains or maybe a signal to us that something inside us needs correcting or some attention. What a wonderful feeling you will get once it is all behind you like the calm after the battle of weather patterns that produced a storm.

The Earth is refreshed, and the grey clouds lifted revealing the promise of peace once more. Move on because there is much good work left to be done, work only you were created to do. Get your fire back and keep pressing forward.

True Grace: Granting the Gift of Time and Space

Sometimes people may need a little time or space when things get tough. Often, we misinterpret this distance as a personal issue they may have with us. Our insecurities will have us believe our loved ones are changing their minds about our relationship or doubting what we share with them. Our anger and offended feelings will tell us to defend ourselves. The old sour grape story comes to mind in this case. "Well," we think, "If they're having doubts about me maybe I'm having doubts about them. Maybe I never really wanted them in my life in the first place." The truth of what we really need in these moments is patiently waiting for doubt, fear, ego and emotions to be cleared out of the way so it can speak. The grace we need waits and releases in its perfect timing. It can only exist when we have placed God, once again, first place in our lives.

Most of us need to let time pass before we allow God to get through. In reality when our loved ones need time, we actually need the same thing – time to get right with God again. Time to talk to Him, worship Him, pray with Him and surrendered to Him. We have focused so much energy on others that we have neglected, if only for a while, our relationship with our Creator. We have been relying too heavily on another human being to fulfill our dream when only living for God can do that. Living for God can do better than that. It can fulfill His dreams for us, which are far greater than whatever we may have planned. Turn your troubled relationship to God. Let Him heal it as only He can. By doing this you free your mind and open your heart to clarity and living fruitfully. You will find peace again knowing that your loved one, in his or her own way, is finding that safe haven too. You are both rerouting back on track to what will work and last in the long run.

We love as only humans can; it is only God who loves completely. It is only God who we can trust to love and accept us with no conditions or subconscious issues attached. With Him there is never the fear of being misunderstood. Allowing them time to get right with God is one of the most loving things we can give to someone. After all, don't we want the best for them? When they are sick, don't we want the best doctors and medicine? When they are lost, the best teacher or instructor? Who better than God to heal and guide? What a blessing to love someone enough to let him or her run away from you and into the arms of our Savior. He knows the sacrifice it takes to let go and promises to restore to us what we turn over out of love. He sees our faith in action and this must make Him proud that we are His.

No Spoilers Possible

A number of people I know are curious about the supernatural or psychic realm. They read books on such phenomena and look at the stars for guidance. They are constantly searching; asking why, when, who and how? At times when they talk, I sense the fear in their voices even in their excitement. Something is not quite right. They begin to change their lives according to predictions and premonitions all the while anticipating, wanting and waiting. Where is the peace or calmness that faith brings? The faith that needs no proof, visions or explanations has been substituted as if it were not enough.

How joyful it is to have all the answers in our faith. What childlike freedom it feels like to not know what the future holds minute-to-minute or day to day but trust that we will be cared for always. To be surprised by the butterfly, a tickle or a rainbow. What joy to meet blessings at an unexpected hour! How sweet to find love where you least expect it. To welcome life just as it is unfolding, wonder and all.

Though it is good to search out goodness and wisdom, true contentment comes in remaining calm in the care of a loving God who will cradle you close regardless of what the future holds. Once a friend who had recently lost her job said she would feel better if she could just hear a psychic tell her everything would work out alright. How sad, I thought, that she couldn't recognize that she already had that promise from God. Who can be a better source than the Almighty? His miracles are new each morning. We are His beloved children and He has nothing but good things planned for us. He never charges a fee because in His great love for us He has already paid the price for these gifts through the sacrifice of His Son. He only asked that we honour this sacrifice and trust Him and only Him.

There is nothing to be gained by looking where we are not yet destined to look. I believe we know exactly what we need to know when we need to know it. There is order in the universe, a wonderful loving order that will reveal itself in good time. That is why I feel one of the most nurturing things a parent or any of us could do for a child is to believe. When we model this peace and joy, we are teaching little ones it's alright not to know all the answers. We can only see in part but we know all parts work together for our good. Regardless of the state of the world, God is in charge.

I heard someone say once that they did not know what the future holds but they know who holds their future. What comfort this belief can bring to the recently unemployed, to the sick, to the lonely and the afraid. God has our best interest in mind. Our blessings are being held and released according to His great plan for our lives. This divine order is difficult for us to understand but taking time to review our lives and how things have worked out just as they should have, helps testify to this truth and encourage others. Eyes up! God is the answer we are searching for always. Living according to His Word will never steer us wrong. Don’t doubt, but instead in all matters and at all times, believe.

Confessing

When I was younger, I could recall being taught about this miraculous thing called confession. You enter the confessional with sin and left renewed. You were rid of all the naughty lies you told and other no-noes. For the most part, I did feel relieved and forgiven after confession. Unfortunately, that fresh feeling did not last very long. I soon found myself falling into the same old routines of impatience, gossip, anger and other types of misbehavior. I remember being so disappointed with myself. Here I was confessing the same things again since my last visit. I even felt ashamed to return to confession. God must be so frustrated with me. I was such a hypocrite. I felt that I was lying to God directly in my praying that, “I would avoid the near occasion of sin”. I felt like I would have to avoid life itself to keep that promise! How wrong it must be to confess a promise in all likelihood I would not keep.

It was not until I met one priest in confession that my spirits were lifted. Upon hearing my concerns about being a repeat offender, he gently reassured me that the worst thing that we could do to God was to turn away from Him for any reason. That was, in fact, the real definition of sin. Real sin is to turn away from God. What a revelation! In not feeling worthy to approach Him with my confession I was turning away from Him. In keeping away I was jeopardizing remaining in and falling deeper into this state of sin. My shame was depriving myself of His forgiveness and care. When I failed, I needed to own it and declare it so it can be removed as the obstacle that kept me from living within His presence. I was never to deprive myself, or God, of that kind of intimacy again.

I have learned to own my missteps more quickly and then I am able to run to God for restoration that realigns my life back on track with less repair needed. If we can admit we have made a mistake quickly, it helps to then better correct that mistake or prevent the further damage it can cause. As we do this more often, we may even be able to catch ourselves before we slip into negative behaviours or actions. This is how we grow and mature in our relationship with Christ, ourselves and with others.

At times my confessions are more formal but more often they are a quiet and private conversation between me and God. Gentle and sincere. When preparing for confession it helps to ask what the matter is. What is troubling us? What has gone off course or has been neglected? What essentials in our lives have we forgotten? Have we forgotten to be patient, to be available, to give rather than receive? It is when we take the time to focus and clear things up that we can remember. Yes, I feel like confession is really a remembering. It's all about remembering who we are and Who loves us. It is when we forget these truths that we become miserable, lonely and confused. This is the true heaviness of sin. The key is to remember, admit and release. Release these burdens to God who loves us. God waits for us to come to Him with everything. Come to Him alone in your room, or on a walk or in a confessional. He is always so thrilled to forgive us. He knows what you have done, He only waits to erase it.

Prayer for Repentance

Dear God, I'm sorry. I've been hurting lately but I know you've been hurting more. When I stop to think of how petty I've been, I'm ashamed. But I do not want to have this shame separate me from you. Please forgive me. I'm so sorry. You suffer through every ounce of human pain in the poor, the sick, the scared and the lonely. I am sorry for: (insert what is on your heart).

Believe me when I say I want to change no matter how many times I failed you before. Help me to take steps towards You and Your plan for my life, and in doing so, let me make a difference. I pray for forgiveness from those I've hurt, I've disappointed and I've forgotten. To my friends, my family and everyone to whom I closed up to; I pray that they will not give me up. However, if the do I trust it is all part of your plan. You, my Lord, have always taken me back unworthy though I have sometimes been. Help me to see myself more as how You see me. In the faces of people, I come across may I see my neighbour. In the eager eyes of children, may I see the future, the truth and the goodness I so want to preserve and nurture. When I see my foe in the distance, I know You call me to pray for them most of all. Thank you for being patient and kind. I promise I'll try not to disappoint you or me or the world by choosing to withhold the gifts you have meant me to share. Fear and insecurity will not have their way. I will be triumphant over sin by becoming closer to You. Amen.

Forgiveness

A while ago, I remember feeling so tired, angry and sad in the midst of a challenging time. It was the loneliest I ever felt. I found myself crying and feeling like with every tear whatever joy I had left was leaving me. Replacing it was a cold dark emptiness I hope to never know again. I tried busy myself with silly things; cleaning, reading, eating, writing, painting even shopping. Every time the dark feeling would be there, ever-present waiting to occupy my mind again. The one

I love was far away. For whatever reason I was left alone silenced and neglected. I was angry I knew that much. I was sad too but preferred the anger to the sadness; less painful you see but just as toxic.

Finally, night arrived, and I lay in bed looking at my window. Tired, quiet and still I cried the tears I had fought all day long. I rested my head on the pillow as if on God's very shoulder. Then I asked Him, “What do I do?”. The answer came quickly. As if waiting all day to be asked God answered, “Pray”. Just as quickly as the word came to me, I entered into prayer. The beautiful calm tone returned to my voice. I stayed meditating for a while in the verses that I spoke. My feelings were clear and my anger under control. Was I still frustrated? Yes. Lost? Definitely. I was hurting too. My heart had been tested to a limit it had never reach before. Needing further counsel, I spoke to God again, “Help me please. Stop this awful anger and ease my heavy heart”. From somewhere, in my ears, in my soul, I heard His voice again. “Only you can help yourself right now. Only you can do what needs to be done.” What on earth could I do that God couldn't, I wondered. Then just as those thoughts entered my mind He responded, “Forgive.”

“Forgive”. The word stopped me, silenced me and captured me. “Forgive”. I sat with this revelation and breathed it in. The wisdom of the word hit the very core of me. I knew once again how Mighty God is. How real and how present He is. This one word was the key to my salvation. It's power at the brink of my very own lips all along. In my wilderness of hurt, offended feelings and tired heart I could not find it. I could not fathom it or access it. For certain, I was getting further and further away from it with every negative thought that occupied my mind. But yes, I needed to quite simply, forgive. I had spent hours analyzing, theorizing, debating, strategizing and complaining and now God had put me right. It was clear that it was my choice. He could not make it for me. He could not bring this healing. I had to choose it. I had to activate it.

Then in the silence of this same night, after serious contemplation, I spoke the words, “I forgive you”. I spoke to the one who hurt me intentionally or not. The offense didn't matter the forgiveness did. There it was some of the most loving and powerful words ever to spill out of my soul. I knew it meant everything. In that quiet moment I was humbled. My heart became warm again, my breathing cleansing leaving me still and peaceful. The anger was gone.

I knew I had to remember my forgiveness and visit it often to keep it true. That would mean abandoning all offense and all bitterness. It would mean refusing the pull of pride and the nagging of insecurity. This would be difficult, yes, I knew that, but I had what I needed. Light would be there to help me, prayer there to train me and my God there to love me through it all.

Sabotage or Victory, You Choose

"How come I have to be the one to... Fill in the blank."

"Why is it always me who... Fill in the blank."

"I'm tired of being the only one who... Fill in the."

Do any of these questions sound familiar? Do you catch yourself asking these questions often but having read them out loud now was very difficult? Seeing them written down really makes them clear. It sounds an awful lot like whining. I know because I catch myself saying the same things too. Until I remember that, my will and what I want can't always be the point. We live for a bigger purpose. One that is so big it remains out of our perspective; it simply doesn't show up on our radar.

We can wonder all we want but the answers will never come before their time. No matter how much research, precious time and effort we put into figuring things out it is sometimes only more confusion that we find. The mystery will be solved as the clues presents themselves. In the meantime, it is our duty to remain alert, positive and strong. This way we are ready to maximize the blessings when they arrived. Sitting around moping and complaining will only delay our reward. This only postpones the blessings God so eagerly want to give us today. Imagine being the biggest saboteur of your own dreams or being the primary conspirator against your own destiny. You, the only obstacle to paradise. Just like Adam and Eve we have it all, but we throw it away every day for what? Because we are impatient? We choose to listen to lies or fear mongers. We invest in hours of worry, doubt and anxiety. How we need to change.

Clear out the dust and garbage from our lives so that the glory of God could be revealed. Shake off those nasty habits. Delete the negative messages from our minds. Let us straighten and strengthen our bodies. Let loose the addictions that plague us and hold tight to the legacy that is ours. We were created for greatness! If we have to live through hard times, let us not become hardened. If we have to get our hands dirty, let's do so without having the dirt stick. We must remember that we are anointed. If suffering is upon you do not let it be within you. Remember this too will pass. What is trying is only temporary, but our reward is eternal.

It is so easy to throw in the towel and run away from our greatness. The enemy would like nothing better than for us to diminish our own potential and extinguish our light. Remember we are *that* necessary in life. We are *that* influential and powerful and it is this that makes us a threat. Do not let tests and setbacks discourage you. Refuse to believe the lies. Let us remain certain that all will work out for our good in the end. You are lovable and capable and with God's help no one could stop you, not even yourself.

Let your Guard Down and Let your Life be Lifted Up

It always amazes me at how some people think they have it all under control. They carefully manipulate and maneuver. They over analyze and overreact. All in an attempt to protect or glorify themselves. They cling to their ability to control others, and every situation involving others. Never realizing that they are robbing themselves of everything that really matters. Their relationships can never be deep because true connections cannot be made without vulnerability and humility. They strive to be one step ahead of everyone without realizing they are falling marathon lengths behind. They are chasing an image of success that is hollow and isolating. What they fail to realize is the following truth. There is a sacredness to being open to letting your life unfold. A sacredness that may require letting go and exposing yourself to others and their opportunity to take advantage of you or hurt you. But should this happen, you will not be hurt for long as you will be lifted above as others try to pull you under. It is they that will feel the biggest blow and you will have been their teacher. You see, pain may be inevitable but healing from these attacks builds resilience. It creates a connection to the brotherhood and sisterhood of others who were unfairly treated before us. The Bible teaches that, “Blessed are you when people insult you, persecute you and falsely say all kinds of evil against you because of me.” (Matthew 5:11). And in knowing this truth, we are indestructible, unshaken. They not only fight a losing battle they are fighting a lost one. “It is finished.” John 19:30.

I understand that nobody likes to feel embarrassed or humiliated or taken advantage of. But sometimes those experiences are all part of our journey of protection or promotion. In many cases, we can choose to feel embarrassed or humiliated. If someone intentionally is hurtful towards us, that is on them. It is not on us. Why should we own that embarrassment or humiliation? If we are prideful, we feel these emotions a lot more than people who are not so proud. The humble person is the person who understands their worth in the eyes of God. They do not need praise. Most of all they do not need self-praise. They also trust in a God who is loving towards them, so loving towards them that He always wants the best for them and that He is always looking out for them. So much so that they don't have to look out for themselves as God Himself is fighting their battles. In an attempt to control every situation, what people think of you or how you come across (stronger, smarter, prettier, richer, etc.) fails in comparison. Having a strong self-sense of self as a child of the Almighty allows us to be able to relax into our future. We brag in the Lord and how we are loved by Him we don't need to brag any other way.

People who choose to live in the rat race with endless competing and manipulating have been blinded to believe they are rodents, not radiant. I just think of how exhausted they must be. They are always needing to be right and never admitting when they are wrong. Apologizing is good for the soul. Always assuming the worst in others means those negative intentions must have first crossed your mind before you put them on another. They live rejecting truth choosing to live in instead in their own false narrative or false reality. They rob themselves of their inheritance and their anointing. They reject the gift of family and friends who only want the best for them and only want to be a good thing in their lives. They fail to accept the blessing of others who were placed in their circle to enhance their experience and aid in their journey. It saddens me so much that people would shut out the very people who were divinely selected for them. Instead, they choose a vacant and narrow way of life with no room for anything that does not pass their approval.

My prayer is that they make a change so that they could have rich and full lives in the truest sense. I hope they choose to enjoy the people that God has placed in their path for a divine purpose, reaping the harvest of the knowledge that they want to share, of the love that they offer. The very fulfillment that they hunger for is only a relationship away. The healing they need blocked by their own defensiveness. I remain hopeful that sooner than later they will realize that meekness is strength. That humility is one of the greatest virtues anyone could possess. My hope and wish and prayer for them is they realize that they are robbing themselves of the ultimate victory. They are denying themselves what God himself died to give us. Freedom, joy and peace.

So, if you own some of this need to control or mistrust, please own it and release it immediately. There is no more time to lose. Accept another way. Accept a beautiful way of sweet surrender instead. A life of quiet confidence and endless victories to battles that truly matter. Your life will be lifted and blessed in ways you never could have imagined or calculated. You must be exhausted Beloved; stop. You were not designed to live like this. You were designed to live in the light of God's glory not your own.

Precious Peace

We have been taught, and teach our children, to be nice to one another. Sadly, this is too often not the case. I don't know why people hurt other people. In our workplaces and schools, countless courses and workshops focusing on coping strategies for toxic relationships are becoming the norm. Conflict resolution strategies, how to deal with difficult people, respect in the workplace and harassment seminars are just a few examples of some courses I personally have attended. This being said, I have yet to attend a lesson that really advises as God does.

"We are often troubled, but not crushed; sometimes in doubt, but never in despair; there are many enemies, but we are never without a friend;
and though badly hurt at times, we're not destroyed." (2 Corinthians 4: 8-9)

Sounds pretty reassuring, doesn't it? The teaching of God guarantees the time-tested essentials; Peace, Faith, Forgiveness, Healing, Joy and finally remembrance of our inheritance, which includes all these blessings and more!

It can be challenging not to take what someone is saying about you or doing to you personally, but we just can't let it stick. It can be especially hurtful when the attack or rejection is coming from someone we care about. We feel misunderstood and try to clear up any misunderstanding with no success. At times the very thing that we are being accused of is the last thing we would ever conceive of doing. The truth is none of what is happening during confrontations like these has to do with us. They rarely have to do with what they say the issue is either. Ultimately, hurt people attempt to hurt others. Their unresolved pain is governing their actions. Their past offenses do not excuse their current bad behaviour but somehow some people feel these past or current hurts give them a licence to lash out or attack others. It is all a distraction from doing the work they need to do to heal.

This has been one of the most challenging lessons I have had to learn and relearn. When reflecting on what is happening or on what we are accused of, it is important to own what we may have done (intentionally or not) and apologize. Once we have done that it is imperative that we let the rest go. It is not our fault that there is something wrong with them. I think I need to repeat that. It is not our fault that there is something wrong with them. If we can see this simple truth we can refuse to be villainized, shaken or moved. Their negative feelings will not be perpetuated in us. We will be able to recognize the pain, anger, and wash our hands of it. A shield will form, and its shiny armour will serve to reflect those negative feelings back to the source. Maybe then, the initial instigator of the conflict will recognize his or her garbage and clean it up once and for all.

People will say awful things about us, the key is to never agree with them. Don't buy what they're trying to sell. Don't match their fire for fire – extinguish it. Don't win or lose the game simply refused to play. Let them rage war, you- keep your peace.

Respect Our Differences for We are all the Same

I believe that now more than ever the gap between churches and religions is narrowing. There is so much to gain by opening up to different perspectives. We will soon discover that the message is the same. The love is the same. It was not until a few years ago that I first started expanding my readings to include other spiritual insights and lessons. The first time I finished reading a great inspirational book, I was surprised to discover that it had been written by someone who did not share my specific religious background. But it was certainly clear that they shared my beliefs.

God created us all to be so unique and just as there are different ways of learning there are different ways of receiving God's teachings. An educator will often use different teaching techniques to present a lesson for they know that their students will require it for their success. This is done in an attempt to cover all the bases and present an environment of learning with the maximum amount of retention potential and solidify understanding. Should you hear something that does not fit with you however, shake it off and move on. We are not called to judge, fight or try and correct everyone. Living open and accepting to others' beliefs may challenge us but we will be left comforted and reassured.

It is like this with the lessons of life. God will use all that is at His disposal to maximize our ability to grasp the important concepts of living. Some of us will be more receptive in a synagogue, others in a mosque or church and others in fields of wildflowers. Hearing from God manifests in many different ways. Responding to His calling on our lives is a unique experience and that is part of what makes it so sacred. Worshiping becomes customized to everyone's individual relationship with the Creator. We give and serve in the unique way that our experiences and gifts guide us. Some people are extremely gifted at reading and interpreting scripture, others devote hours to prayer and meditation. Others still, praise through their artistic talents, by preaching and others by offering quiet support. God knows how unique we are; He created us. He recognizes our every effort to become closer to Him.

When we choose to get caught up in our differences, this only distracts us and impedes our growth. We all have a responsibility to live each day doing our best. For all that this requires we need to stay close to the only one who can make that possible and follow His example. When the disciples of Christ felt the need to defend and segregate themselves from other groups Jesus was quick to correct them. "Do not try and stop him, Jesus instructed his disciples in regard to another preacher, because no one who performs a miracle in my name will be able soon afterwards to say evil things about me. For whoever is not against us is for us. I assure you that anyone who gives you a drink of water because you belong to me will certainly receive his award." (Mark 9: 39-41).

We miss the point when we judge or squabble. God is good in any language, in any country and at all times. We are all on the road to enlightenment and salvation. Certain people and events contribute to that sacred journey. How loving it is to allow in whomever God has sent to teach us. He knows what He is doing and how to do it. It is our place to let Him work. Our hearts will recognize the messages intended for our good. They will resonate within us and we will know the value of their teachings. Regardless of whose mouth the words come out of, we will know that it is God who speaks as soon as we hear Him.

The Good and Gentle Shepherd

Do you ever notice how many mistakes and goof-ups you make when your boss is around? You suddenly become clumsy, and tongue twisted second-guessing your every move and decision-making abilities. You are obviously capable of doing your work but for some reason the presence of an intrusive employer makes you begin to question your competence.

My guess is that workplaces and communities with more supportive administration and leadership are not only more enjoyable but also more fruitful. This has certainly been the case in all the places where I have worked. Communities with positive leadership and initiatives become just that, communities. We are honoured to become many parts of a working whole. In those environments nothing matters more than people. There is a mutual respect between all its members who feel safe enough to take risks and aim higher. Think about how liberating it feels to be trusted; to have the confidence of a superior that you will succeed. Your heart rate decreases, your mind is clear, you are motivated and you find joy and peace in your work. You are able to activate creative energies and as a result, others reap the blessings of your investment.

God is like that. He is our Good Shepherd that looks out for us. He trusts us, believes in us and knows we are capable. He is never invasive or critical, instead He is patient, ever waiting and always believing. God knows that there is much work for us to do but He has entrusted this important work to the most competent candidates. He has placed all the skills, gifts and abilities in us so that His work can be done just as He meant us to do it. No other person has our exact duties to perform. No other person has our exact experiences, qualities or testimony needed to fulfill and complete the mission God has set before us. He qualifies us.

God doesn't watch worried or doubtful as we work. He just simply loves us. Waiting to supply whatever we may need. Ever ready to replenish our energy, inspire our minds and renew our spirit. With that support, we can return to work every day clear with our vision sharpened. We may lose sight of our focus and question our purpose but God never does. He knows it isn't easy, all He asks is that we firstly and always trust in Him. He will reveal our purpose. Every time we complete a task or perform a good deed that feeling that enters our heart will be proof enough that we are on track.

So, the next time someone tries to push you around, or if you find yourself dragging your feet, remember who you really work for. Remember who truly promotes and protects. Remember that you are valued. With this new perspective, you could fly through your nine-to-five with your head held a little higher knowing that this too is part of the plan. God is the ultimate project manager and His projections show a prosperous outcome. What an honour to work for We must learn to look at the bigger picture and always love what we see.

Appreciate the Sacrifice and Proclaim it's Worth!

I have come across many people who believe the only way to worship effectively or obtain favour with God is through sacrifice. I once saw young man on television, who was searching for direction in this life by carrying a large wooden cross across town. Hasn't Jesus done this already so that we would never have to? Is this not the exact thing He died to prevent? Does this glorify God? No. This is an extreme example but how many of us, in some other ways, are doing the same thing?

How about when we are critical of ourselves, listen to negative self-talk or focus on slip ups and mistakes? Are we not torching ourselves this way? How about when we withholding forgiveness for ourselves until we feel our sentence has been served? This cannot be the way.

God wants us happy. This is what glorifies God. We are to “walk and not faint”, (Isaiah 40:31). We are to be victorious, strong, blessed and joyful. We are to represent. It is easy to escape into a world where salvation could be bought because maybe then you think you can redeem yourself. We have been redeemed. We have been saved. This truth can seem too much. It is easier to believe the lies that tell you, you are not deserving of God's love and that you have to earn it and suffer to gain it. The truth is you are precious and loved unconditionally just as you are now. Find the courage to believe, that you will heal, laugh, jump, and play. Shake off whatever makes you hesitate to trust this for this is the way of the Lord. You are needed here strong and healthy. You are called to great works here and now. This sounds bold but it is this boldness that allows us to take steps towards God. Otherwise, we are stuck in a place where we can become vulnerable to deceit and temptation. Together with God we are healers, leaders, instruments of peace and all that He requires of us. Ultimately, it is this trust and faith that requires courage and gains reward.

This by no means suggests an easy life. Oh no, the life I just described can be a challenge. It is hard to be happy. Harder even than gruelling rituals and self-inflicting torment. It takes true courage and sacrifice to smile when you feel like crying. Just like the exhausted single mother who fakes a smile each night before checking your kids into bed or the father who works in freezing cold temperatures for poor wages to make a living for his family. I know a woman who is recovering from breast cancer and still makes it to her volunteer job at the community centre to help those less fortunate. This is what activates blessings in our lives. And God sees them all. Forgiving when you have every reason to hold a grudge. To choose God’s victory over self-pity. Meekness over self-praise. These types of sacrifices honour God for they are fruitful. They produce resilience, fortitude and honour. They foster connections to others that are divine and unbreakable. They testify of God's Goodness and Great Plan.

There are so many examples of good mothers, fathers, doctors, firefighters, counsellors, teachers, volunteers and so many more people who live in love at all time. Let this be the gauge in which you measure your coordinates. Let love be the key in all you say, think and do. May it be in your speech and in your actions. May love be everything above you, below you, before you and behind you. This will help you remember your sins are forgiven and your rewards are here on earth as well as in heaven. Real devotion is to display a positive and grateful attitude at all times. It is hard to pick ourselves up and declare our holiness. It is hard to demand the rights of our inheritance and live in joy. Yes, some days it is hard to believe that we are worthy and blessed. Nonetheless we do not let what is hard trap us. You are valuable to life. You are valuable to God.

Decide today to live the glory of the blessings God has given you. Your ransom has been paid. The ultimate sacrifice already laid down for you. Honor that love by soaking up all the beauty in the world around you. Prove to the world that God's sacrifice was worth it. Rejoice and be thankful!

Water from the Well

We have all hear the experts preach about the physical benefits of drinking water; but I wonder what water does for us spiritually as well. Fish tanks can be found in medical and legal waiting rooms in an attempt to calm anxious patients and clients. Restaurants have fountains or similar fish tank to promote relaxation an add to the ambiance. Spas offer aqua therapy treatment like soaks and floats. The sound, smell and sight of the ocean waves inspire so many. Water connects us to each other. The other day when I was out for a walk on a particularly still evening, I could hear the rush of water beneath the streets from the grates and was instantly mesmerized by the sound. Oceans bridge the gap of geography and link continents. Rivers and lakes join villages and towns. The energy of each waves carrying the hurts, joys, troubles and victories of all mankind exchanged through a constant watery flow.

In the Bible, we find water as a recurring symbol. Jesus often preached by the water side. He took walks and retreats by the many bodies of water around His home. He is first introduced into society as an adult while being baptized in the Jordan River. Shortly after, when it came time to look for his first followers, Jesus set out towards the sea and called upon fishermen. In order to perform His first miracle all Jesus needed was water. Through His calming of a raging sea, He showed us the power there was in trusting Him. Finally, by asking an outcast for a drink by a well He taught us acceptance and forgiveness.

The community well was a place of social gathering and central to life back in Jesus's day and is still the case in many places around the world. My parents actually met and fell in love at the village well. But I digress. When Jesus spoke with the Samaritan woman at the well, He knew she was troubled and searching for spiritual satisfaction. She was most likely tired of the same routine of collecting water needed for her many chores and the demands of an outcast's life. When speaking with her, Jesus took the opportunity to incorporate water with his message of renewal, connecting this women's physical depletion with her spiritual one. In asking her for a drink of water He was showing her that she had a purpose and a choice. He was asking her for assistance and she could choose her next move. She was worthy of more and if she chose to change her life, she would receive everything she ever needed. How welcoming this idea must have been. How wonderful to be replenished so fully and continually. To be offered a remedy to the mondain, the rejection or the sorrow.

This depiction of water as freshness, cleanliness and rejuvenation can be applied to us today. Let us allow this message to wake us spiritually every morning as we splash ourselves awake at the sink asking ourselves what we need to clean. On a hot summer day when there is nothing that quenches our thirst more than a long crystal, clear drink of water let us ask ourselves what our souls thirst for. When a sudden rain storm hits, let this be a symbol of what we may need to release or let wash away. When we unclog the kitchen sink may we recall the importance of unblocking what is preventing us from accepting the flow of God's love and blessings for us. Remember, if you will, this story of the woman at the well and take time to drink the Living Water Jesus described so your true resources will never dry up!

Love Lessons

Having been blessed with nieces and nephews and now, great-nieces and great-nephews, has really taught me so much more about God's love. It has been a gift to watch them grow and to love them every step of the way. I still see them so little and feel their chubby little arms embracing my neck as I cradled them. Is that how God holds us in His heart I wonder. There are no favourites. They are all favourites. There is no comparing the uniqueness of people. It must be this way with God, we are all His favourites. They have helped me understand so much more clearly what love is all about. It doesn't matter how many mistakes they make or I make, Love remains. That special connection and devotion to another person is undeniable and unbreakable.

When I was younger and would trip up; like lose my temper, gossip or slip into another bad habit I would feel so unworthy of turning to God for forgiveness. I knew that He was the only source that would restore me back into balance but still I was ashamed to go to Him. As an aunt the worst thing one of my (great)nieces or (great)nephews could do is not come to me when they need me. Sometimes they'll make a comment before approaching me for advice and say something like, "I just don't want to bother you again." I wish they understood that anytime they share with me is always a complete and total honour to me. How much more must God feel appreciated, honoured and joyful when we turn to Him at all times.

The funny thing about children is that no matter how much it may appear we help them grow they help us grow twofold. Loving them when it was easy and the rare times when it was difficult, proved to me that at all times we are called back to the love we share. It is the closest thing to unconditional love that I have ever felt. I thank them for that gift and I pray that they'll always realized how much all of them have meant to me and continue to mean to me. I will never stop fighting for them. I will never stop choosing them. I will never stop being interested in them no matter what turns their lives might take. I have watched how their God given talents and qualities have perfectly suited them for the callings and challenges in their lives. I have seen how God loves them more than I do and am taught of how so much greater that love must be then our human ability to love. I am forever thankful to and for these special young people that God has gifted me with as family. May they always know how much I love them and how they continue to teach me about God's great love as well.

Triumph in Survival

There will be days when everything that could go wrong, will. When the weather forecast calls for sunny skies and then the clouds roll in. When you are just getting out ahead of the game and your called back down into the minors. Life presents a number of these challenges, stretching our patients and testing our faith. The reason why these bad things happen is really irrelevant. The key is to survive.

And survived we do. Somehow these difficult times find their way behind us. They become a chapter in our story and part of our testimony. Like the time I remember being scared and sick, too weak to even walk. The nights never seemed so cold nor the days so long. There was little comfort offered from doctors who could not pinpoint an exact problem. My mind, which always found good company in books or creativity was tired. The only thing that remained was the promise of my faith. Somehow, I knew that my life was on surveillance. Somewhere God was watching me and working to heal me again. Little things became big things as I savored every footstep and moment without pain. Music, rest and breathing became crystal clear, refreshing and healing. The hug of a tiny baby who smiled and remembered me, called me to remember myself. I began to declare, "I am not sick but well able. I am not diminishing; I am rising up. I am not little, I am big; so big that even my imagination could not fathom my power. I had things to do with my life and people to serve. I was not defeated I was needed."

With this awakening message playing in my soul, I could begin to cross the barrier placed before me. I could begin to push my way through the darkness and turn my face towards the light. To begin this challenge, I would need one thing… the belief and acceptance that I was loved. The moment I realize this truth to my survival, I began to recognize love everywhere. I felt love from family members and love from the singing birds. I felt love from the words in a poem and the devotion in a prayer. I nursed myself with love from the Earth by eating the food it had grown enriched with vitamins and energy. The landscape around me offered me love too as it smelled of flowers, soil and rain. Oh, the blessed rain! It loved me in that is dissolved all the impurities and flushed away all the offenses. The loving sun pulled me out of doors to refreshen my lungs and the cool air in the night provided shelter and calm. I listened for hours to silence for what was expected and I heard the same message…the belief and acceptance that I was loved.

Today I stand in thanksgiving, I dance in gratitude, and I remain in faith. God heals all things at all times, times that are right for us more than for Him. If you are facing a challenge and are hurting, sick or lost, I pray for your recovery and enlightenment. I pray for the healing of your body, the healing of your mind and the healing of your heart. I believe in your triumphant survival and offer you the lesson I learned- you are loved.

Today I Needed to Paint

Well, I guess I'm writing today for a reason although I haven't quite figured out what that reason is it just yet. It has been a good day. I stayed relatively busy or should I say more importantly I was relatively productive. I ate right. I painted. Oh, that's right, I painted! I hadn't done that in a long time. I knew the restlessness within me needed a creative out. So, I pulled out the paints and brushes then sat before the empty canvas and began.

First, I pulled out a sky from the blobs of white and blue. Next came the grass smooth, fresh and green. A road found its way into my landscape, bumpy, rich and right. Then, to brighten and let the world know God was there, I added flowers. Tiny splashes of colours tucked here and there were just the signature pieces I needed to wrap the whole scene together. Kisses they seemed. Yes, special kisses filled with love. That is how God must sign His masterpieces.

The song on the radio while I painted was so much like a prayer. “Have I Told You Lately That I Love You?” I imagine saying the words to God. I know what you're thinking, God is all knowing He must know that I love Him. But think about it. The ones who love us; we know they love us but still we are thrilled when they tell us so. When they take the time to stop what they're doing to think of us and reach out and make that connection, we are reassured once more of the special bond that is shared.

How God's eyes must fill with tears of joy that His child has remembered Him. His heart so heavy with the pain of sin, can for a moment recognize the love for which He died. His mother too must be glad as well as the angels and saints for all their works and sacrifices are renewed by our faith. Yes, God knows that we love Him. But how great His Joy must be when one of His children reaches up amid all the devastation, all the hurts and disappointment, and see through to a greater place. They can see a bigger picture that comforts and calms. They can feel the special existence and attempt to honour it with picture, song, prayer or painting.

I guess I needed to paint today. I needed to reconnect to the beauty of life. I needed to remember. I needed to relate to God in a different form of prayer or meditation. It felt great to spend the time with Him as I painted. I wasn't frustrated or rushed but focussed and peaceful. I intend to remember this form of worship in the future and hope to please the

Great Master with my amateur portrayal of His greatness again sometime soon.

In Conclusion

Upon revising my final draft for this book, a passage from the Bible came to my attention. I felt it was appropriate and deeply meaningful and so will sign off with these words in a letter Paul wrote to the Romans. Thank you once again for reading with me and may God bless us.

"Love must be completely sincere. Hate what is evil, hold on to what is good. Love one another warmly as Christian brothers, and be eager to show respect for one another. Work hard and do not be lazy. Serve the Lord with a full heart of devotion. Let your hope keep you joyful, be patient in your troubles, and pray at all times. Share your belongings with your needy fellow- Christian, and open your home to strangers.

Ask God to bless those who persecute you – yes, ask him to bless, not to curse. Be happy with those who are happy, weep with those who weep. Have the same concern for everyone. Do not be proud, but except humble duties. Do not think of yourselves as wise.

If someone has done you wrong, do not repay him with a wrong. Try to do what everyone considers to be good. Do everything possible on your part to live in peace with everybody."

(Roman 12 9-18)

Made in the USA
Middletown, DE
25 August 2021